AF228644

ULTIMATE SPORTS STATS

PRO BASEBALL

BY THE NUMBERS

Percy Leed

Lerner Publications ◆ Minneapolis

Lerner Publications Company
An imprint of Lerner Publishing Group, Inc.
241 First Avenue North
Minneapolis, MN 55401 USA

For reading levels and more information, look up this title at www.lernerbooks.com.

Main body text set in Adrianna.
Typeface provided by Chank.

Designer: Viet Chu

Library of Congress Cataloging-in-Publication Data

Names: Leed, Percy, 1968– author.
Title: Pro baseball by the numbers / Percy Leed.
Description: Minneapolis, MN : Lerner Publications, [2025] | Series: Ultimate sports stats (Lerner sports) | Includes bibliographical references and index. | Audience: Ages 7–11 | Audience: Grades 4–6 | Summary: "Sports fans love to compare stats, and no sport has more to discover than baseball. From wins to home runs to earned run average, explore baseball's most important stats and their significance to the game"— Provided by publisher.
Identifiers: LCCN 2023037417 (print) | LCCN 2023037418 (ebook) | ISBN 9798765625927 (library binding) | ISBN 9798765629857 (paperback) | ISBN 9798765638088 (epub)
Subjects: LCSH: Baseball—Records—Juvenile literature. | Baseball—Statistics—Juvenile literature.
Classification: LCC GV877 .L34 2025 (print) | LCC GV877 (ebook) | DDC 796.357—dc23/eng/20230814

LC record available at https://lccn.loc.gov/2023037417
LC ebook record available at https://lccn.loc.gov/2023037418

Manufactured in the United States of America
1-1010065-51926-12/14/2023

TABLE OF CONTENTS

NUMBERS GAME

Baseball's stories have always been told through statistics (stats). Fans use stats to compare players with one another. Teams use stats to study the game and improve. The sport has had three distinct eras. Conditions during each era affected baseball stats and the ways fans view them.

DEAD BALL ERA

During MLB's Dead Ball Era (1900–1919), home runs were rare. Ty Cobb led the American League (AL) in 1909 with nine home runs. Compare that to another Tigers slugger. In 2012, Miguel Cabrera hit 44 home runs to lead the AL.

MIGUEL CABRERA

Live Ball Era

In 1920, baseballs began to be made with a new yarn that helped them fly farther. Banning spitballs and other changes also led to more scoring. Babe Ruth of the New York Yankees did his part too. In 1920, he hit 54 home runs. That was more than any team in the AL hit.

BABE RUTH

Steroid Era

Many MLB players used drugs such as steroids in the 1990s and early 2000s. The drugs increased power stats such as home runs. In 1998, St. Louis Cardinals slugger Mark McGwire's 70 home runs were more than the entire Cardinals team hit in 1991. The league banned steroids but didn't test all players for them until 2003.

MARK MCGWIRE

CHAPTER 1

PLAYER STATS

CAL RIPKEN JR.

NO SICK DAYS

With 162 games each season, MLB teams may go weeks without a day off. Every single game for more than 16 seasons, Cal Ripken Jr. played for the Baltimore Orioles. The record will probably never be broken.

MOST MLB GAMES PLAYED IN A ROW

PLAYER	FIRST GAME OF STREAK	LAST GAME OF STREAK	TOTAL GAMES
Cal Ripken Jr.	May 30, 1982	September 19, 1998	2,632
Lou Gehrig	June 1, 1925	April 30, 1939	2,130
Everett Scott	June 20, 1916	May 5, 1925	1,307
Steve Garvey	September 3, 1975	July 29, 1983	1,207
Miguel Tejada	June 1, 2000	June 21, 2007	1,152

TONY GWYNN

SWING, BATTER, SWING!

Batting average measures how often a batter gets a base hit. Batting .300 means a player gets three hits every 10 at bats. Hitting .400 or better has been done dozens of times in MLB history. But it has not happened since 1941 when Ted Williams batted .406 for the Boston Red Sox.

HIGHEST FULL-SEASON BATTING AVERAGES SINCE 1941

YEAR	PLAYER	TEAM	BATTING AVERAGE
1994	Tony Gwynn	San Diego Padres	.394
1980	George Brett	Kansas City Royals	.390
1977	Rod Carew	Minnesota Twins	.388
1957	Ted Williams	Boston Red Sox	.388
1999	Larry Walker	Colorado Rockies	.379

WAIT, WHAT!?

In 2014, Jose Altuve led the AL in batting average. At 5 feet 6 (1.7 m), he was the shortest player to lead a league since Wee Willie Keeler in 1898.

JOE DIMAGGIO

CHASING JOE DIMAGGIO

Despite hitting .406, Ted Williams did not win the AL Most Valuable Player (MVP) award in 1941. It went to Joe DiMaggio. Why? The New York Yankees outfielder got a hit in 56 straight games that season. No one has ever come close to matching DiMaggio's incredible streak.

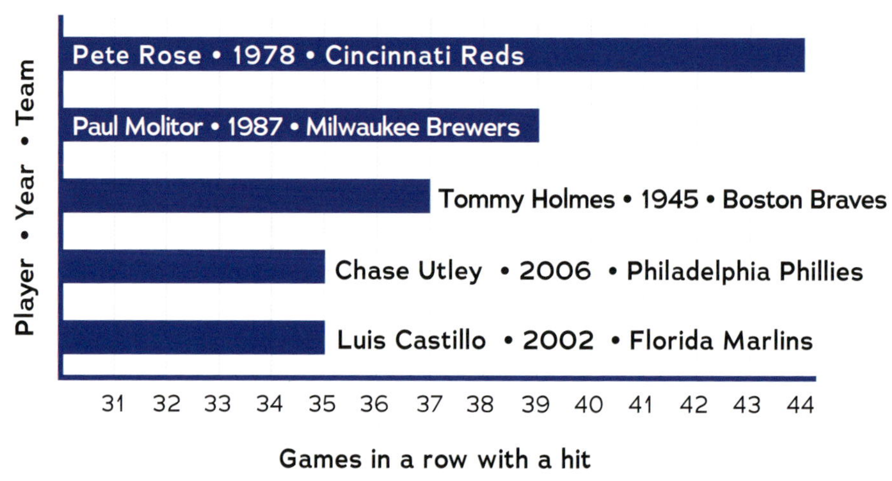

THE HIT KING

Pete Rose couldn't match Joe DiMaggio's 56-game hitting streak. But Rose claims a famous MLB number of his own: 4,256. That's the most career base hits. It took a long time to get there. Rose played 24 seasons, mostly for the Cincinnati Reds. His 3,562 games played are the most in baseball history.

ALL-TIME HITS LEADERS

PLAYER	HITS
Pete Rose	4,256
Ty Cobb	4,189
Hank Aaron	3,771
Stan Musial	3,630
Tris Speaker	3,514

BARRY BONDS

In 1927, Babe Ruth swatted 60 home runs to set a new season record. That magical number stood for 34 years. Yankees outfielder Roger Maris topped Ruth's record in 1961. Maris's new record of 61 home runs lasted 37 years. Then, during a four-year stretch in the Steroid Era, Maris's record was topped six times.

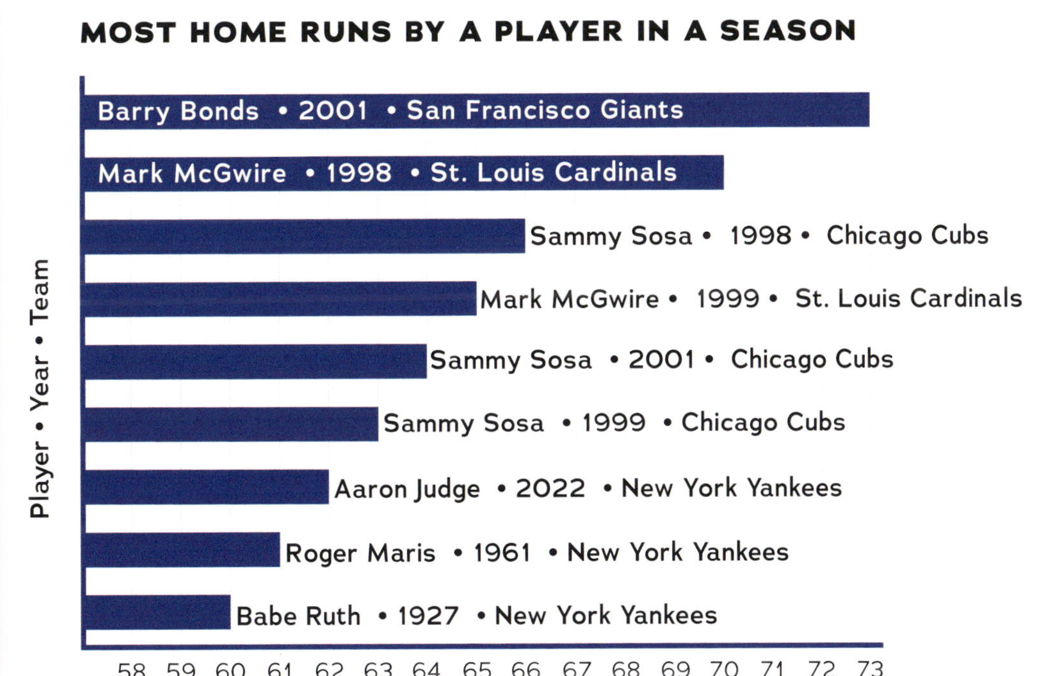

MOST STOLEN BASES IN A SEASON SINCE 1900

YEAR	PLAYER	TEAM	STOLEN BASES
1982	Rickey Henderson	Oakland A's	130
1974	Lou Brock	St. Louis Cardinals	118
1985	Vince Coleman	St. Louis Cardinals	110
1987	Vince Coleman	St. Louis Cardinals	109
1983	Rickey Henderson	Oakland A's	108

WAIT, WHAT!?

In 2023, MLB made several changes to the game. One of the changes was making bases 3 inches (7.6 cm) larger. The larger bases made stealing bases easier.

PITCHERS WITH 20 OR MORE WINS IN A SEASON SINCE 2018

PLAYER	YEAR	TEAM	WINS
Kyle Wright	2022	Atlanta Braves	21
Justin Verlander	2019	Houston Astros	21
Blake Snell	2018	Tampa Bay Rays	21
Spencer Strider	2023	Atlanta Braves	20
Julio Urías	2021	Los Angeles Dodgers	20
Gerrit Cole	2019	Houston Astros	20
Corey Kluber	2018	Cleveland Indians	20

Everyone Makes Mistakes

Fielders sometimes make errors that lead to runs. Earned run average (ERA) shows how many runs a pitcher allows that aren't the result of errors. The stat is one of the best ways to tell how a pitcher really performed.

STARTING PITCHERS WITH THE BEST SEASON ERAS SINCE 2000

NATIONAL LEAGUE

YEAR	PITCHER	TEAM	ERA
2018	Jacob deGrom	New York Mets	1.70
2020	Trevor Bauer	Cincinnati Reds	1.73
2014	Clayton Kershaw	Los Angeles Dodgers	1.77

AMERICAN LEAGUE

YEAR	PITCHER	TEAM	ERA
2020	Shane Bieber	Cleveland Indians	1.63
2000	Pedro Martinez	Boston Red Sox	1.74
2022	Justin Verlander	Houston Astros	1.75

Wait, What!?

In 2020, the disease COVID-19 spread around the world. To help avoid spreading COVID-19, MLB shortened its 162-game season. Each team played only 60 games.

KENTA MAEDA

MORE WHIP, PLEASE

WHIP stands for walks and hits per inning pitched. If a pitcher gives up a hit and a walk in an inning, the WHIP is 2.00. Good pitchers usually have a WHIP between 1.00 and 1.50. In 2000, Pedro Martinez's WHIP of 0.74 broke an MLB record that had lasted 87 years.

STARTING PITCHERS WITH THE BEST SEASON WHIP SINCE 2000

YEAR	PITCHER	TEAM	WHIP
2000	Pedro Martinez	Boston Red Sox	0.74
2020	Kenta Maeda	Minnesota Twins	0.75
2020	Trevor Bauer	Cincinnati Reds	0.80
2019	Justin Verlander	Houston Astros	0.80
2022	Justin Verlander	Houston Astros	0.83

YOU'RE OUT!

Nolan Ryan struck out 5,714 batters in his 27-year MLB career. That's nearly 1,000 more than anyone else. But Ryan never struck out every batter in a game. No one has. A team has 27 outs in a nine-inning game. Only four pitchers have reached 20 strikeouts.

MOST STRIKEOUTS IN NINE INNINGS

YEAR	PITCHER	TEAM	STRIKEOUTS
2016	Max Scherzer	Washington Nationals	20
2001	Randy Johnson	Seattle Mariners	20
1998	Kerry Wood	Chicago Cubs	20
1996	Roger Clemens	Boston Red Sox	20
1986	Roger Clemens	Boston Red Sox	20

MARIANO RIVERA

Relief pitchers often enter close games and record saves. Saves did not become an official MLB stat until 1969. Of the 31 relief pitchers with 300 or more career saves, all of them pitched in the 1980s or later.

CAREER SAVES

TEAM STATS

JUST WIN, BaBY

Winning percentage can tell you how many games a team will win if they keep up the same pace all season. Teams that win six out of 10 games have a winning percentage of .600. That equals about 98 wins in a full season.

BEST SEASON WINNING PERCENTAGES SINCE 2020

YEAR	TEAM	WINNING PERCENTAGE	RECORD
2020	Los Angeles Dodgers	.717	43–17
2022	Los Angeles Dodgers	.685	111–51
2020	Tampa Bay Rays	.667	40-20
2021	San Francisco Giants	.660	107–55

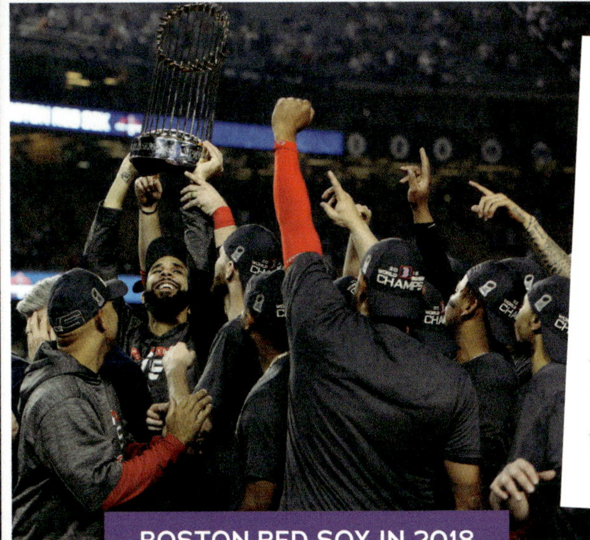

BOSTON RED SOX IN 2018

eye ON THe PRIZe

The 2001 Seattle Mariners led MLB with a .716 winning percentage. But they didn't reach the World Series. To judge a baseball team's history, the most important stat is World Series championships.

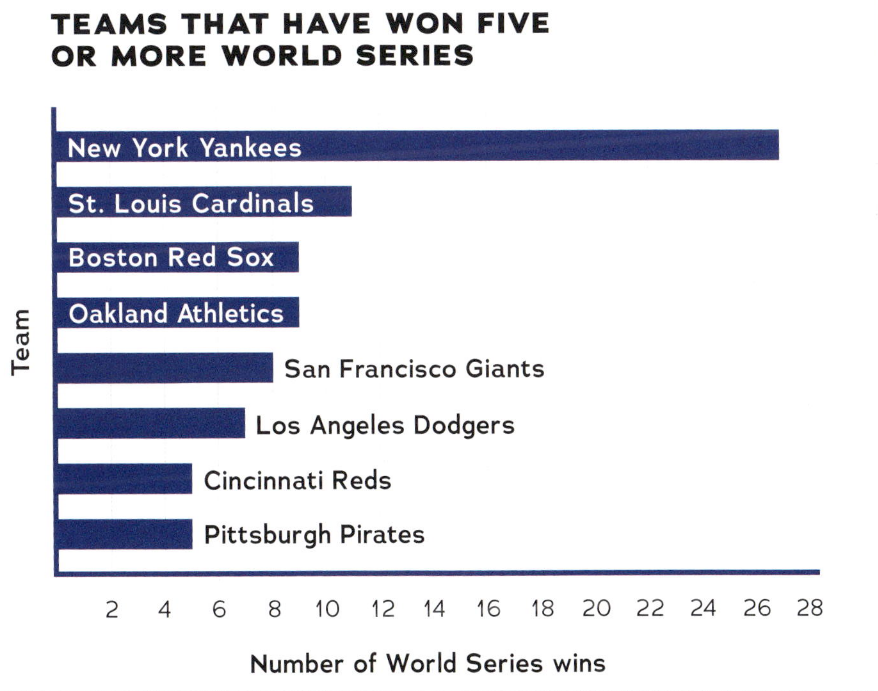

Sometimes MLB teams catch fire! Long winning streaks can help teams catch up in the standings. Or a streak can help a team win a championship.

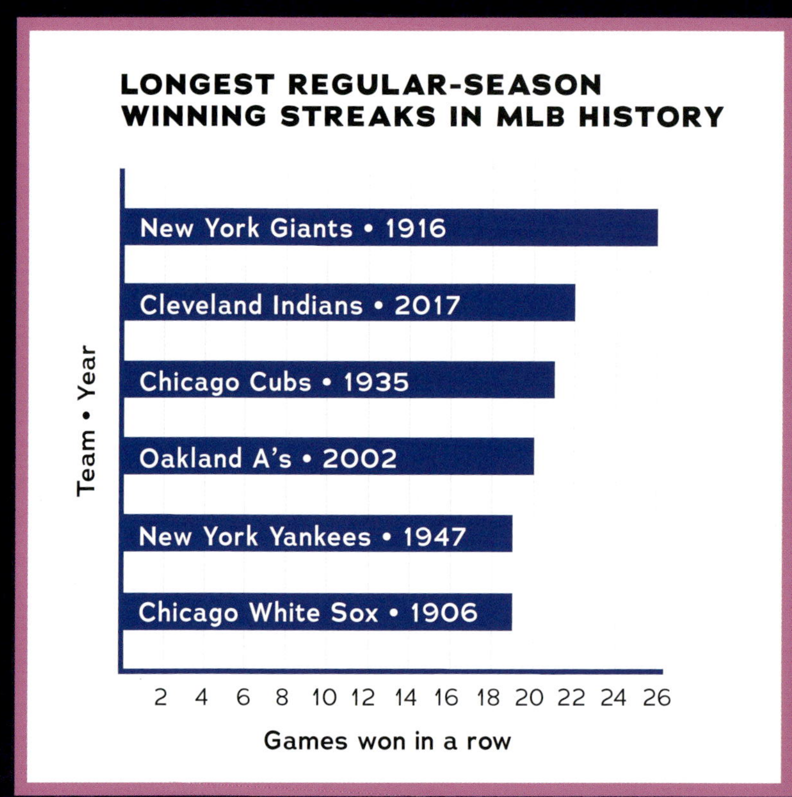

WAIT, WHAT!?

In 2023, the Tampa Bay Rays tied an all-time MLB record. They won their first 13 games of the season. It was the longest winning streak in Rays history.

GREAT COMEBACKS IN THE STANDINGS

Comebacks are exciting! Your favorite team may be just a winning streak away from glory.

2022 The Philadelphia Phillies finished the season 14 games behind the Atlanta Braves. But the Phillies reached the playoffs and beat the St. Louis Cardinals, Braves, and San Diego Padres. The Phillies finally lost in the World Series to the Houston Astros.

2011 The Tampa Bay Rays were nine games behind the Red Sox in September. The Rays passed the Sox on the final day of the season by beating them in extra innings to claim a playoff spot.

1969 On August 13, the New York Mets trailed the Chicago Cubs by nine and a half games. The Miracle Mets wound up beating the Cubs by eight games.

1964 The St. Louis Cardinals were in fourth place in the National League with about a month to play. St. Louis got hot and took over first place on the last day of the season.

1951 The New York Giants were 13 games out of first place in the standings. Then they won 39 of 47 games to claim first.

TONS OF HOME RUNS

When baseball began in the 1800s, there weren't many rules to keep games fair. Spitballs and other tricks made batting a chore. With more rules and better equipment, the Dead Ball Era died, and home run rates rose.

NELSON CRUZ
WITH THE 2019
MINNESOTA TWINS

FEWEST TEAM HOME RUNS IN A SEASON

LEAGUE	YEAR	TEAM	HOME RUNS
American League	1908	Chicago White Sox	3
National League	1917	Pittsburgh Pirates	9

MOST TEAM HOME RUNS IN A SEASON

LEAGUE	YEAR	TEAM	HOME RUNS
American League	2019	Minnesota Twins	307
National League	2023	Atlanta Braves	307

Hall of Fame

It is a great honor to become a member of the National Baseball Hall of Fame. Only 270 former players have made it. In 2023, baseball writers voted on 28 players who could make the Hall of Fame. Only third baseman Scott Rolen earned enough votes to enter. First baseman Fred McGriff also entered as a special selection.

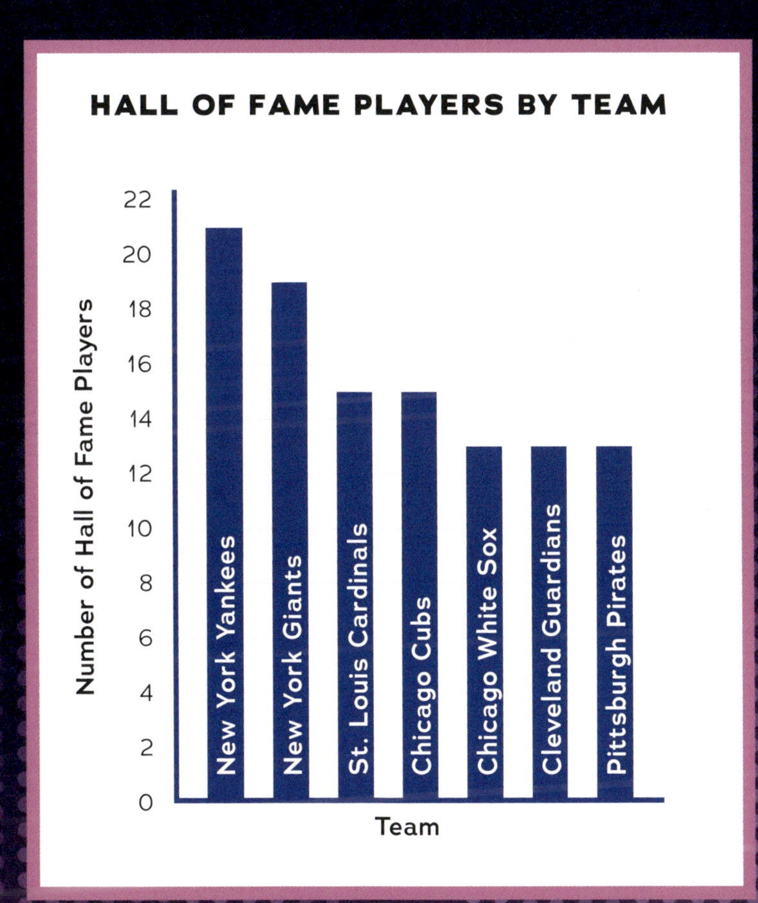

STATS ARE HERE TO STAY

HENRY CHADWICK

Baseball has changed a lot since the 1800s. But how fans read stats hasn't changed much. Sportswriter Henry Chadwick created the box score in 1859. You could write a full-length story about a baseball game by studying this table full of numbers. But first, you need to know how to read it. Use the keys to read the box score on the next page from the final game of the 2022 World Series.

BATTING KEY
AB = at bats
AVG = batting average
BB = bases on balls (walks)
H = hits
R = runs scored
RBI = runs batted in
SO = strikeouts

PITCHING KEY
BB = bases on balls (walks) allowed
ER = earned runs allowed
ERA = earned run average
H = hits allowed
IP = innings pitched
R = runs allowed
SO = strikeouts

HOUSTON ASTROS BATTERS

	AB	R	H	RBI	BB	SO	AVG
José Altuve	4	1	1	0	0	2	.250
Jeremy Peña	4	1	2	0	0	1	.500
Yordan Álvarez	4	1	1	3	0	1	.250
Alex Bregman	3	1	1	0	1	1	.333
Kyle Tucker	3	0	0	0	1	1	.000
Christian Vázquez	3	0	1	1	0	0	.333
Trey Mancini	3	0	1	0	0	1	.333
Chas McCormick	3	0	0	0	0	2	.000
Martin Maldonado	2	0	0	0	0	0	.000

HOUSTON ASTROS PITCHERS

	IP	H	R	ER	BB	SO	ERA
Framber Valdez	6	2	1	1	2	9	1.50
Hector Neris	1	0	0	0	0	2	0.00
Bryan Abreu	1	0	0	0	0	1	0.00
Ryan Pressly	1	1	0	0	0	0	0.00

GAME ACTION

Fans and players love to study baseball stats. Pitchers use stats to plan their pitches. For instance, a pitcher might be more careful with a batter who has a long hitting streak. Batters may change the way they swing the bat based on the pitcher's stats.

Managers use stats to decide where fielders should stand. With a power hitter at bat, the manager could have the fielders play farther back than usual.

Fantasy and the Future

Fantasy baseball is a game that fans play with stats. To play in a fantasy league, fans choose players to form teams. Fantasy teams are ranked based on the stats of the players. One study showed that nearly one in five adults in the US plays fantasy sports.

The use of numbers in baseball will likely grow. As players and managers study stats, they make changes to the game. It will be fun to see where stats take baseball next!

Ronald Acuña Jr. of the Atlanta Braves and Juan Soto of the New York Yankees are two of baseball's biggest superstars. They both began their MLB careers in 2018. Fans love to compare them and argue about which player is the game's best.

RONALD ACUÑA JR.	
At bats	2,626
Hits	767
Runs	543
Triples	11
Home runs	161
Batting average	.292
Stolen bases	180

RONALD ACUÑA JR.

Here are their career stats through the 2023 regular season. Who is the better player? It's up to you to decide!

JUAN SOTO	
At bats	2,704
Hits	768
Runs	527
Triples	11
Home runs	160
Batting average	.284
Stolen bases	50

JUAN SOTO

GLOSSARY

earned run average (ERA): the number of earned runs a pitcher allows in a nine-inning game. To calculate ERA, divide the number of earned runs by the number of innings pitched and then multiply by nine.

error: a mistake made by a fielder that allows a batter to reach base or a base runner to advance

manager: the head coach of a baseball team

save: a stat for a relief pitcher who finishes a game by recording the last out with a lead of three runs or fewer

slugger: a powerful batter

spitball: a pitch thrown with a ball that has saliva or sweat on it. A spitball moves in unusual ways and is hard to hit.

steroid: a harmful drug that can make athletes stronger

stolen base: when a base runner takes a base without the ball having been hit or an error made

WHIP: short for *walks and hits per innings pitched*

Learn More

Anderson, Josh. *Aaron Judge vs. Babe Ruth: Who Would Win?* Minneapolis: Lerner Publications, 2024.

Baseball: Statistics
https://www.ducksters.com/sports/baseball/statistics.php

Calcaterra, Craig. *Stars of Major League Baseball.* New York: Abbeville, 2023.

Fishman, Jon M. *Baseball's G.O.A.T.: Babe Ruth, Mike Trout, and More.* Minneapolis: Lerner Publications, 2020.

MLB Stat Leaders
https://www.mlb.com/stats/

National Baseball Hall of Fame
https://baseballhall.org/

INDEX

PHOTO ACKNOWLEDGMENTS

Image credits: Steven King/Icon Sportswire/Getty Images, p. 4;
Transcendental Graphics/Getty Images, p. 5 (top); SPX/Diamond
Images/Getty Images, p. 5 (bottom); Ron Vesely/Getty Images,
pp. 6, 7, 10; Photo File/Hulton Archive/Getty Images, p. 8; Focus On
Sport/Getty Images, pp. 9, 12; Patrick Smith/Getty Images, p. 13;
Brace Hemmelgarn/Getty Images, pp. 15, 22; Mitchell Layton/Getty
Images, p. 16; Justin Edmonds/Getty Images, p. 17; San Francisco
Chronicle/Hearst Newspapers/Getty Images, p. 18; Boston Globe/
Getty Images, p. 19; The Sporting News/Getty Images, p. 24;
Carmen Mandato/Getty Images, p. 25; Icon Sportswire/Getty
Images, p. 26; Xavier Lorenzo/Moment/Getty Images, p. 27; Thearon
W. Henderson/Getty Images, p. 28; John Fisher/Getty Images, p. 29.
Design elements: Ali Kahfi/DigitalVision Vectors/Getty Images;
sarayut Thaneerat/Moment/Getty Images.

Cover: AP Photo/Peter Joneleit/Icon Sportswire.